This Is How You Survive

LANA RAFAELA CINDRIC

DEDICATION

To my parents, who raised me to be free.

And to all those who believed in me.

Thank you.

CONTENTS

ACKNOWLEDGMENTS

A big thank you to the designer of this book's cover and a close friend – Bethany Climpson. Thank you for reading my mind and my thoughts.

I owe my eternal gratitude to Jéssica Rabello for being my second pair of eyes with 20/20 vision. Thank you for your brilliance.

And thank you to everyone who has stood by me. To my family. To my friends. To my readers. It means more than you know.

LANA RAFAELA CINDRIC

PREFACE

Recently, a friend told me that she associates the feeling of throwing the middle finger at your past and doing your own thing with who I am as a person and as a writer.

If that is the case, it is because there has literally been a point in my life where I said: Well, shit, after everything that has happened, I have two options. I can either wait for the next thing to hit me and then survive that, or I can choose to push back and thrive. And for me, there is no version of reality where I am able to carry the weight like a stupidly overcrowded suitcase that doesn't fit in the overhead compartment. I am my own pissed off flight attendant.

So I really did flip that middle finger at the past and said: fuck this. Fuck whatever is stopping me from living any way I want to. This fear that has been instilled into so many of us? Not enough to make me stop. I am not tragic, I am so fucking full of life that I am bursting at the seams. I deserve better.

And so do you.

This book? This book is here so you know that you are not alone.

I hope these poems give you comfort and strength and enough righteous anger to go out there and make a choice.

Do the pain's thing, or do your own thing.

And you know what?

We all deserve better than to be grasping for straws in our own lives.

I. RUIN

But I am tired of trying to understand what the universe means when it carves another scar into my back.

I am tired and I just want to come home.

ATLAS LOST

Your shoulders ache from all the weight
you have been carrying.
You are not Atlas because he, at least,
knew that the burden was not his to bear.
You became one with it.

Dreams become kaleidoscope splinters that cut
your fingers and send shivers down your spine.
Maybe you've lost it somewhere along the way,
taken a wrong turn at a crossroads.
And maybe you have been roaming all along.

In the dead of night,
when the absence of hope
presses its heaviest on you,
something kicks in.

You fight with your hands pressed against the walls
and you push until you have forgotten that
humans
were not supposed to bend the bars
of golden cages.

And under the burden,
you start to sing.

In the darkness,
you devise your own light.

BELONGING

You grow as a collage:

You are bits and pieces of other people,
taped together and assembled
like a nightstand from the dollar store,
(poorly,
parts missing,
no reclamation).

So you say:

I'm sorry but some days it's hard,
some days I don't know what is me and
what is someone else's tragedy.

I'm sorry but some nights it takes all of me
to rearrange the parts,
put myself together from scrap,
like a replica that could never match the original.

I'm sorry but what I am trying to say is that I am
part tragedy, part comedy,
a dash of joy and a pinch of misery.

And some nights,
I don't even know if these bones
are mine.

WINGS

Things which are *free* are rarely beautiful.

You say *wild* and mean woods,
sunlight through tree canopies,
feet planted on the ground.

                    You say *wild* and mean
                              tame.

I say *success* and you see a throne,
your body never big enough to fit it,
brocade and marble.

          The crown on your head has been set on fire
                              and yet,
                         you smile.

     Oh, the things we fool ourselves into thinking
               when we feel small.

If your heart could speak, it would tell you to fuck off.

When have you ever come for advice?
Brain and reason know best.

               But they don't know anything
          about why you have grown *wings*
                    and still can't fly.

THESE WORDS ARE BIRDS

At night, I write slam poetry in my head
and damn, that shit is *wild*.

Here is how I can speak in rhythm,
how I open my mouth just so -
the words flow so easy but they are birds
when I try to put them on paper -

and it hasn't occurred to me until just now
that it might be fitting.

At night I write slam poetry in my head
and I wonder what our metaphors
are gonna look like in twenty years.

Someone once decided that things should be pretty;
be pretty when you cry,
be pretty when you stumble,
be pretty when you write and *please*
don't turn another poem into revolution and blood.

I know that you grew
eating up the tales of dead revolutionaries
and that is how you saw a full heart;
a body bleeding in the streets, blood to gutter,
gutter to sea,
sea to stars,
just a man just a woman just a child and I wish,
I wish I didn't have to write this
but that's just how it is.

This is how it always was and I wish
I could write about starlight
but whenever I do
it is very hard because being soft -
it doesn't come easy to me
so I string metaphors that I try to make pretty
(don't make it a revolution don't make it rubble
and don't make it a bomb,
don't make it heavy hearts, be light be soft –

Be pretty.)

My head is a cathedral sometimes and it echoes,
not with the old men who told me that I am never
going to heaven
if I like the way you spoon fed me absinthe and fueled
my dreams with soft hands and made me feel good,
feel light like happiness is a bubble in my chest -
but steel, too,
and it is not going to burst -
I understand this now.

My head is a cathedral because this is where you come
to pray
when there is no hope.

Be pretty and yes, alright,
dye my hair blonde, smile more
even if I hate my teeth,
press my lips to his mouth, unhook -
oh no, not this time,
some lines you can't uncross.

When I was sixteen, I cried over myself
in a bar slowly filling up with smoke -
a lifeboat filling up with water and the moment
when you realize that your last chance of salvation
is long gone.

When I was eighteen, I knew what hope
and defeat
felt like,
and how porcelain sounds so good
when you smash it.

So what I am trying to say with this broken tongue,
with this soul out of place,
is that at night,
I write slam poetry in my head
and my fingers are full of rings and I look good,
I do not look pretty, I am *wild*,
I am wild and I am a tempest and I will
draw you in,
into the blue and into magic and madness
and it *will* feel like coming home.

What I am trying to say is that at night,
I write slam poetry in the cathedral
of my own making,
forging stories and myths about the man
who loved the world so much -
even when it didn't love him back,
and maybe I am trying to learn from him.

At night, I write slam poetry in my head,
in my cathedral in my bed and
it hurts like freedom
and I don't look pretty, but I look happy,
no rings on my fingers to show that I live
and breathe
my art,
but I'm getting there.

At night, I sleep in my poetry.

At night, metaphors are August nights
and I don't carry mountains on my back.

At night, I am just a girl
with my feet in the ocean
and I don't know what pretty means,
I don't know what holy means,
I don't know why your words are wind chimes
and mine are war drums.

At night, I wasn't born because of a war,
with a war,
and I do not end in a war.

At night,
this poem just ends with a smile.

THE ALCHEMY OF BROKEN THINGS

These flowers bloomed out of nothing and *now*
you expect me to want your gold?

Listen, you don't know about caged animals,
how we'd rather gnaw our legs off than be kept
captive, you don't understand what a shackle is
until it has stopped you from running.

No one starts with 'listen' or 'wait' or 'so' unless
they are backed into a corner
so
here I am, palms open, my heart on plate, and listen,
I *am* backed into a corner - always have been, I know
what it means to hit a wall
and walk away with scars.

Good news: I don't need your gold.

Flowers bloom, that is just what they do but I am not
a flower so when my mother brings me roses for my
birthday, I laugh; I am not a flower, you know me,
you *know* I have claws – damn, you have scars to
remember them. I am an inferno, can't you see that?
You don't leave wreaths for fires.

They'd just burn them, anyway.

A boy doesn't bring me flowers because I am not
the type, they always know, I always laugh too loud
and gifts to these goddesses are cigarettes and less
loneliness, more loveliness – never flowers.

They'd just burn them, anyway.

And so I do not grow as a flower - I have no roots,
I have no leaves, I have no petals to blossom with.

But *I bloom*.

By God, do I bloom, and I bloom like every wretched
thing who has ever been told that she will never
amount to anything more than ash.

So today I don't need your gold.
I sprouted from the pavement, from the weeds, from
the ugly.
My knees are already dirty,
I know the alchemy of broken things.

And your gold?

I'd just burn it, anyway.

UNFINISHED

We can't be growing
when we are still just
patching holes,

praying that the flood
does not wash away
what we barely saved.

So I am not sorry for
being pretty
in all the wrong ways.

While you were building,
I was burning.

- So don't ask me why I'm stuck in an infinite
loop, don't ask me why I am more tempest
than soul some days, don't ask me the question
lodged in your throat. I am tired of answering
your questions. I am tired of the emptiness
that comes after a storm and the world never
gave me anything anyway. I don't owe it a
damn thing. Not even an explanation.

LIKE HONEY

Here is what you do:
You fight.

You fight for your place on Earth,
you fight for your breathing air,
you fight to be alive
and you fight to stay that way.

You fight even when your knuckles are bruised,
when you spit out the blood in your mouth
and ask: *Is that the best you can do?*

You fight even when you are trying to be kind
but the world is cruel,
you fight to be soft and
for your smile to drip like honey.

You fight when you love,
two hands holding onto salvation,
you fight to stay
even when your bones scream to leave.

You fight because every now and then,
you drop your gloves to the floor,
tap at the mat, call for a timeout,
and laugh.

And when you laugh, baby,
hurricanes stir in your eyes
and every chuckle is a forest fire.

Because, when you laugh,
you laugh because you are alive.

And then you fight some more.

YOU ARE WHAT YOU CHOOSE TO BE

You weren't born in a thunderstorm and
the heavens didn't shake
when you let out your first cry,
but you learned how to make lightning out of nothing
and you shook the heavens all on your own.

So maybe you weren't born into a crown,
maybe you are as soft as the first day of spring
and maybe your smile can stop wars,
maybe you don't think you have it in you
to keep fighting.

But here is what I know:

Roses grow thorns,
nature is kind but doesn't forgive,
and you are a warrior
even though sometimes it hurts to breathe.

A TRAINWRECK

If they are looking for a trainwreck,
they are not going to find one here.

No,
you fought to be whole.

You screamed at the universe
to heal the cracks in your heart,
fill them with starlight,
make them more than this ache.

And it just whispered back:

You can't fix something that was never broken.

FROM RUINS

Look,
some nights pain weighs on you like a ton of bricks
(empires built on your breaking back).

I know, baby,
I know what it means to collapse out of spite and
light the first match,
bring Rome down and the world with it.

I know it's heavy and I know your crown has
more thorns
than diamonds,
but you have got to breathe.

You have got to breathe and slow it down,
because this is a flood and this is a forest fire,
this   is   every   single   drop   of   blood
on the arena floor.

But if you have to throw your hands up in the air,
don't do it out of defeat.

Do it for the triumph.

THIS POEM IS A RESCUE MISSION

You ever try opening a Coke bottle but the cap is
on too tight
and suddenly you feel weak without knowing
what the hell you're feeling weak for?

It's like this –
I wash glasses because I can't wash the sadness off of
me and sadness is this humidity clinging to my insides,
etching a hole in my heart and
I feel so small, small, *small.*

It's like this –
I put the glasses in the cupboard
(this is not a pretty metaphor, these are just glasses)
and they sound *so loud* when they touch each other;

I forget where the two plates go and now I hate myself
because I was just washing the dishes, damn it,
and now I'm having a damn existential crisis
in the middle of my kitchen;
Shit, I just wanna be saved but this is the Wild West
and I have to be my own outlaw and my own sheriff.

It's like this –
I can't explain the anger coiling in my stomach
to people who have never felt it,
or how sometimes everything is too loud and this is
not a classroom – it's a circle of Dante's hell,

I can't explain *why* it took me ten minutes to find
the right pen for this poem
or why I like imagining the California highway with
my windows down,
why I know *who* I love because they make me feel
quiet in a very crowded room,
what it means to turn all that boiling blood into ink.

So I write this poem because I am tired and because
I want to be saved,
because I used up all the red and the blue and
laughed through tears in the face of my sadness
(it wants me to choke on saltwater
but I've always been stubborn).

It's like this –
When I was young, I wanted to be free
so I drank up the stars and walked on thorns.

Now sadness' shackles rattle but the stars are still
louder
and this time,
when they tell me how to save my life –

I listen.

NAMES

I'm not good with pretty words and
finding excuses to call an apocalypse
a rebirth.

Violence is violence,
and blood runs red
no matter what we call it.

And maybe you need a helping hand
to turn this ruin into a palace,
but it is always going to be a ruin
and it will *never* be the best of you.

So you collapse,
and that's alright, baby,
we all do, sooner or later,
you get to be a ruin today.

You get to dissolve into nothing,
you get to stand and call your despair ugly,
you get to walk away.

I am not going to call your apocalypse a rebirth,
you deserve better.

WE DRANK UP THE RAIN BUT IT DIDN'T SAVE US

Here is how it happens:

I step off the back of my friend's bike and
nearly burn my calf off on the exhaust.
I'm the cocky asshole you'll love to hate
and the words drip purple down your chin.

I drink them up
like I've been thirsty in the middle of a desert
for a century now
and you smile because you know
what that tastes like.

You said you've got a pair of boots, your guitar
and not much else.
You wear the fact that you have never belonged
on your sleeve but I run my thumb across your lips
and *oh*,
there's that honey I've been looking for.

I get that, baby, I do, because the only thing I've ever
known
is how to kiss you and make it taste like a bruise,
so when you grip my hips and it's a trick of the light
but I swear,
I *swear* the pink neon just made you
holy.

And it gives me hope -
like maybe this violence made us brave in the end.

You write notes on receipts,
I write apologies on the back of *I love yous*,

We were never going to get that happy ending and
you don't shatter that coffee cup
because you know I hate it,
because you know I can rip your heart at the seams
three times a day
but I'm still afraid of loud noise,
tangle your fingers in my hair and say it'll be okay,
even though we both know it won't.

Here is how it happens:

I am brave and you are reckless,
enough to know that walking under the yellow lights
won't turn us good,
and we're desperate, too,
pawing at each other like we're gonna find
that drop of salvation somewhere.

I know now that loving you was like fighting in a
parking lot;
empty and lonely and aching,
red knuckles and swollen lips,
boys and girls with thunderous hearts,

But you still wanted to be someone who could -
who could take this world apart and make it heal.

So when the rain finally comes down and
you open your eyes,
you're hoping it'll save you

but all it does is hurt.

A THOUSAND SHIPS

I don't think I will be your moving force tonight.

No,
I will be my own.

And I will move mountains.

HOW A HERO IS MADE

I don't need to shout,
my head is a cathedral
and my voice echoes all on its own.

A scene: imagine a girl (imagine plaits, too,
    if you'd like),
 now imagine the shaky legs, the innocence
 which comes from knowing nothing
and wanting everything.

A scene: legends are forged from pain so now imagine
    a hero,
 imagine the ichor in their veins,
 place the world on their shoulders
and clap as they struggle.
Now imagine the hero unchained, the vengeance that
   tastes like justice.
Imagine losing everything
     except for your sword.

A scene: the woods are dark and deep and all of the
nightmares
   come to life,
  the stage is a globe and the windows rattle
prettily but
  no one is going back home tonight,
All the windows are boarded shut.

UNTHAW

in my dreams, i see a man handing out prophecies
on the corner for just a nickel.
isn't it supposed to cost more?
when i was a child, i was taught to think rationally so
the prophet smiles.
how much is a map back home worth?
everything.
everything.
here is my offering for safe passage: all that i do not
need. take the broken bones, childhood loves like
mint and strawberries and the courage to dream.
take the hurricane downpour people and take the
steep hills i could not climb with past lives
weighing me down.
take the man who told me that he is worried about me
*– how can you be so cold, i fear for you – when you
finally fall in love, it is going to hurt. -*
but give me the hurt,
give me his fear like cracked veneer,
good, i want to hurt, i want to collapse into a
shipwreck and sink myself trying to defeat what i
cannot.
good, he should be afraid.
do not fear *for* me.
fear *me.*
the inside of my soul is as chaotic as this poem is and
where they see stars, i see muddy water.

good, stand there and watch me unthaw.
it feels good to burn.

SALTWATER SURVIVAL

Fuck your grief and
fuck your tragedy.

I am going to drop this sorrow
like a piece of
trash,
and it will not make for a good metaphor,
and it will not be pretty.

But neither were the tears,
neither was the hollow
in my chest.

This is saltwater survival.

Water fills my lungs
and I sing.

UNBECOME

- *to unbecome* (verb) – ʌnbɪˈkʌm - to cease existing and to begin again, to fall and to bloom.

Unbecome,

Let your bones turn into deep roots,
let flowers bloom from the dark earth
of all that you do not know how to be.

Unbecome,

In the morning,
the sun will tell you
who it is that you are now.

Unbecome,

And then become something else entirely.

II. RISING

I may be walking on thorns,
but at least there are stars in my eyes.

THIS IS WHY YOU CHOOSE TO FIGHT

Here is a list of sad things:

1.) All the things you wanted to say but never did.
The teeth marks on your lips from trying to stop
the words from escaping. The empty space where
music should be.

2.) Learning the taste of a storm intimately. Knowing
just when something Earth-shattering is about
to happen and just wondering who you are going to
become after this one.

3.) Almosts. Always almosts. Never ifs and never
could-have-beens. Just almost, teasing at the tip
of your tongue, itching at your fingertips. A dream
so close to grasping, slipping between your fingertips
like sand.

This is why you want to give up.

Here is a list of happy things:

1.) All the I-love-yous you've heard and said. Every laugh that you caused. Every child's sloppy smile on the street and a tune you caught in passing but couldn't forget for the rest of the day.

2.) The calm after the storm. Like nothing is ever going to happen again, just your ribs shifting so your heart can grow. Just you and the quiet voice in your head telling you that you survived this and you will survive everything else too. Maybe pain makes us stronger and stranger at the same time.

3.) Always. Definites. Sures.
The assuredness in your friend's hand squeezing yours. The always in the sun refusing to give up its shine every day. The definites in how you will definitely live to see another day, realization found in the darkest hour of the night.

This is why you choose to fight.

ANTIGONE

You are not a tragedy,
and maybe that goes without saying
but I have to tell you.

I have seen the way you laugh and
I have seen you give up the scars,
open your wings even if they are a little messy,
a few feathers missing.

I have seen how you fly so easily,
like there is nothing weighing you down.

That is not a tragedy.

That is someone who shouted
FUCK YOU, GREEK TRAGEDIES!

That is someone who sang
when they ought to have been screaming.

There is nothing more beautiful than the world
telling you that there is
no hope,

and you finding a way to create some,
anyway.

I LOVE YOU

I think it's brave,

I think it's brave that you get up in the morning
even if your soul is weary,
and your bones ache for a rest.

I think it's brave that you keep on living
even if you don't know how to anymore.

I think it's brave that you push away the waves
rolling in every day
and you decide to fight.

I know there are days when you feel like giving up but
I think it's brave
that you never do.

EVERYTHING IS GOING TO BE ALRIGHT
(AND THAT IS A PROMISE)

I am here to tell you that everything is going to be
alright.

We all know about rust and stardust,
galaxies found in your lovers' eyes,
stray magic caught on your fingertips.

Everyone knows what it feels like to have your heart
break,
scraped knuckles and a shaky voice,
the dead of winter in the middle of June.

But that is not what I am here for.

I am here for the taste of coffee and new beginnings in
the early morning,
your friend's hand in yours,
warm nights when you feel like you are on top of the
world
and like you might just be infinite.

I am here to tell you that everything is going to be
alright
not because the world might decide to change one
night,
not because laughter will replace tears,
but because this is what humans do best.

Humans do one thing
and one thing only –

they survive
and they *thrive.*

THINGS WE SHOULD LEARN FROM THE STARS

1.) You will burn. But this pyre of yours will light an entire galaxy.

Is it destruction if it's creation too?

2.) Collapse into yourself. It doesn't matter. Yesterday is light years away and its cold can't touch you now.

Tomorrow is when you shine.

3.) The explosion will shatter your bones and no one will hear a sound. It is alright, stars die quietly, too.

But they get up every single time.

4.) Like stars, burn brighter after you rise.

5.) (Always rise.)

6.) The universe is a dark and vast place but there is always light. Find it.

If you can't find it, be that light.

7.) Make sure that the whole universe knows just how beautiful you are when you decide to survive.

41

CRUELTY AND REDEMPTION

I. Cruelty

There is something very sharp inside of you.

Sometimes the ones you love touch you and you want to warn them, say: careful, there's other people's pain still caught on the shards.

You wonder how it is possible for anyone to look at you and mistake you for someone whose tongue does not cut through hearts.

There is nothing soft about you when you look at your fingers in the mirror. No amount of water can wash them clean. The blood is here to stay.

No one has ever used the color orange to describe you.

II. Redemption

But you wish they would.

Because orange is tangerines and kisses sneaked on top of rollercoasters, adrenaline butterflies in your stomach, and orange feels peaceful, tastes good, coming home after a long day.

Damn it, you want to be that.

You want to be orange and carry those memories on your fingertips, keep the treasures safe for someone who knows how to love them. Wrap the world around your hollow bones like a blanket and forget that you are small.

So you make it your mission to become orange, scream your lungs out just once to taste what it's like to feel so acutely alive that even the sun's gotta smile.

This is what you have: hands stained red.

This is what you will fight for: soul stained sunset.

THE RECIPE FOR SURVIVAL (AND OTHER DREAMS)

You get lost somewhere between staring at your ceiling
and wishing that you were a star,
far away and beautiful and exploding,
and still able to take someone's breath away.

You've got scraped knees,
a box of dreams under your bed and
if there is something you are sure you would kill for –
then it's that,
a childhood memory and a testament that screams in
your voice –
I was here, I was in the gutter and yet,
I dared to dream.

Because you are the 5pm cold sneaking into your chest
when the world is cruel and you are somehow too
small.

You are the 10am summer morning bravery,
the kind that takes you flying from the monkey bars
and laughing when you taste the dirt and the blood
and *the life*.

You are half-dream half-person,
concrete buildings and peach iced tea.

You are everyone who has ever loved you
and you are every bit your own.

So maybe you are a paradox and maybe
you have always been stuck here,
half-wishing, half-falling
between the stars and the dirt but

You kept looking up
until a miracle exploded in your chest,
it wasn't quiet and
it sure as hell wasn't beautiful

but it was everything

and you survived.

ANATOMY OF THE SOUL

I see you bringing yourself down but, baby,
you are made of galaxies and forest fires
and tempests.

You are a dark cloud,
a hurricane,
a wolf running alone.

Nothing beats the iron in your bones and
the stars in your soul.

A REMINDER

Whenever you feel like you are not good enough,
like you are too small, stuck in one place with nothing
to look forward to -
please remember that life is long
and you are still young.

There are so many worlds you have yet to uncover,
so many words to learn the taste of,
so many things that will make you wonder,
nights that will fill your heart up with the feeling of
complete satisfaction – *If I die now,*
I'll have zero regrets. If I die now,
I'll die knowing what the world's smile looks like,
not just claws.
If I die now, I'll have lived enough.

How beautiful it is to be the first line
of a thrilling story,
you are the play
and the audience is glued to their seats.
You deliver these lines and every step you take
collides and spills and arches,
you are so human.

Doesn't it excite you,
to know nothing
and still want everything?

Only you could be that brave
so cling to that courage -
with your teeth if you must.

I wish you were,
but you are not a songbird.

And these songs?

We must sing them until our voices break.

We must sing them
until something beautiful
finds a home in us.

SPREAD YOUR WINGS

Let me tell you something:

No one is going to look at you, broken and shattered
and think –
damn, you are beautiful.

No one is going to come pick up your broken pieces
off the floor
and assemble them into a beautiful whole.

Hell,
even *you* won't look at yourself and think –
I made broken look beautiful.

You know why?

Because all those writers lied to you.

Yes,
all those with their poems of scraped knuckles and
blood dripping down chins,
pomegranate songs and loves that ripped through you
like hurricanes.

Liars.

So you and I,
we are going to make a plan.

You are not going to romanticize days when
your brain tells you to smash that mirror,
you are not going to romanticize the lover who
doesn't understand you
but still writes about you.

Here is what you are going to romanticize instead:

You are going to romanticize the first day of spring,
its gentle hands all over your body,
lifting you up until you are as light as a feather.

You are going to romanticize the tea and honey kind
of love,
no hurricanes,
just sunshine that builds you up from within,
that helps you make it through the worst days.

You are going to romanticize the gentle hands of
a friend in yours, telling you that it is going to be
okay,
because it is.

And don't trust poets,
we're no good,
we love pretending that our jagged edges tantamount
to a beautiful disaster,
but in reality – there ain't nothing beautiful about
shaky hands holding a cigarette
and empty eyes staring at the cracks in the walls.

You know what is beautiful, instead?

Days when you can look at yourself in the mirror and
smile,
scars and all,
music that makes your soul flow like a river,
books that offer comfort,
families flocking together like overgrown birds
to keep you safe and warm,
friends that give you strength when you can find
none,
lovers who make you laugh through tears.

Baby,
from now on
you are going to romanticize healing;

honey dripping down your fingertips,
August nights that stick to your skin,
the day you find your purpose,
long car rides and singing so loud that
no one can shut you up now.

Bad news:
no one is coming to save you.

Good news:
you can save yourself.

UGLY THINGS

You will find the most breathtaking beauty
in the ugly things.

Scars that are maps to faraway times when your pride
was as loud as your heart,
a split lip reminder of being braver than you are now,
a shape of a star on your knee that is the shape of
your heart,
fingertips to the sky, soul to the stars.

You'll find beauty in crooked knees and too long
limbs, all over the place,
reaching reaching reaching,
and never pausing because this world is yours to take
and
who cares if you are a collage of ugly things,
if your teeth aren't straight and if your hair is
hurricane messy (not in a good way but in the best
fucking way there is),
who cares?

You've got a story to tell for every scar, every flaw;
this one is from when I was reckless and young and
wild
and this one you can't see because it was cut into your
skin the first time they stomped on your heart
but you rose, you rose and you kept burning,
been through hellfire and kept walking.

I am trying to say that maybe it's 3am
and you can't sleep,
maybe you feel like your lungs are full of the cosmos
or maybe you can't breathe in at all
(some nights are hard, it's alright, I've got you)
but you're good,
you always were.

You are not a pretty thing,
you don't smile and make the world stop,
but you've got the kind of body that is a map
and it will always, *always* bring you back home.

AN AFTERNOON POEM

God,
you are too much.

How does anyone live with you,
how can anyone compare to the hurricane you keep in
your chest?

Who taught you that breathing isn't breathing
unless you're gasping for air?

Who taught you that laughing isn't laughing
unless you shift a small nebula?

Who taught you that love isn't love
unless it makes you burn and twist and still
leaves you dopey and sated,
smiling through half-closed eyes and feeling,
feeling *so much*?

There is something that breaks in every single one of
us,
turns those beating hearts to grey,
but you haven't lost a single color.

If anything,
you got desperate,
held on to that hope with fragile fingers,
no matter how much your heart hurt.

So how could anyone love you
without feeling like they are not enough?

When you give and give and whatever
it is that you could
take,

you leave on the kitchen table.

THE COST OF ART

The real cost of art?

The real cost of art is your life falling apart
and you finding a safe corner of the world to
turn that ache into ink.

The real cost of art is how blood runs red and
your heart beats out a war cry,
but you turn it into a song slow enough
to stop hurricanes.

The real cost of art are all the tears that have fallen,
all the loves that were forgotten,
all the lives buried under your skin like a memory
that still tastes like cinnamon and purple sunsets,
dancing wildly on the streets of a city you swear
you know,
the real cost of art is letting all of that go.

The real cost of art is accepting it,
pain and all.

The real cost of art is how this isn't going to be
a pretty poem,
but maybe it will make your heart hurt less.

PEACE

Maybe we are all smaller than we would like to be,
and maybe that is good.

I'm playing devil's advocate here but
how beautiful it is not to be a warrior,
how beautiful it is not to be a supernova.

Instead, just a girl laughing at 7am,
shaky hands and a very, very light
heart.

It's easy,
standing with your toes in the sand,
dreaming of sailing the world,
but just feeling the wind tangling in your hair,
knowing that you can just stand here
and breathe.

Not a galaxy being born, not collapsing
with a crown on your head
and the world on your shoulders,
simply existing in this pocket of time,
tiny tiny *tiiiny*
and smiling
like this is it,
this is what I am and this is what is good and –

Screw poetry,
I just want to feel alive.

One day,
your fingertips will leave a mark on this world.

One day,
you are going to know what you came here to do.

But how beautiful it is to be unburdened,
to know that, for now,
you don't have to.

For now,
you can just be.

And that is a special kind of beauty, too.

HUMANITY

I love it when humans are soft.

Just think about it;
you know people when they are at their cruel,
at their competitive,
hearts on fire and minds as sharp
as the edge of a blade.

And then you see them at 2am,
their heads lolling on their shoulders,
heavy eyelids and soft-spoken words.
Like *I don't know what I'm doing*
and *You're so good to me.*

Sometimes humans are too tired to be anything but
honest,
and catch them then,
look at them when they're just raw emotion
and pure, unbridled magic.

Look at them when they see a beautiful photo or a
poem, tagging their friends,
hastily scribbled love notes in the form of
This reminded me of you.

Shakespeare's love sonnets have nothing on them.

And it takes my breath away
because we are all struggling on this planet,
working and exploring and trying - oh, we are trying
so hard.

But we still have the time to
breathe out *I love you*
and mean it.

CHERRY SWEET

I could love you in such a cherry sweet way,
our fingertips stained with childhood memories of
chipped front teeth.

Come over here, let me show you what it's like to love
when you've got nothing left to lose.
No better living than when you know
it won't last forever.

This is the art of loving when you are always leaving.
This is how you wring magic out of the dusty places.
When my lips are all sugar,
when your body is all wet heat,
don't look at my hands.

I am sorry if it feels like ash some days.

Others will be better, I promise.
I will love you with all the grace of
a tumble down the stairs.

So come over here,
let me show you the sweetness that comes
not in spite of pain,
but because of it.

COPPER

I was so moved I
wanted to rip off my
flesh.
This is not me
this is not
I am not copper wire
a mosaic of violent things
car crash overflowing remnants of a life
not my own.
This
is not me.

I was so moved I could
dance.
Picture stumbling feet
shaking hands,
I am more than this flesh - - a light.
I am a light.

I bury my memories in the front porch,
when they pour cement I say
good.
This is not blood.

This is becoming.

III. REVOLUTION

You are so full,
the moon could never compare.

WHY DO YOU WRITE?

Because I didn't have a nickname as a kid. Because I remember what it's like to be unseen. Because every day I see more and more beautiful things and it is enough to make me overflow. Because none of us are alone, not really. Because I couldn't stay angry at the thief who wanted to steal my bag. Because I hate cold coffee but drink it anyway. Because I wake up afraid but live anyway. Because sometimes I see my mother and I want to give her the life she wants to give me. Because I can(not) forgive my father for how similar we are. Because I can love everyone I hate and I don't even hate them, not really. Because a man selling magazines for the homeless charity told me I am beautiful and I wanted to cry. Because I remember various July heats but I never thought my fingers would reach gold in September. Because I hate neon. Because I love neon. Because I have so much blood on my hands, so much starlight on my hands, because I don't know how to not be polar opposites. Because I don't know how I got this strength and because I will spend my life searching for the formula. Because I was sixteen and when my friend asked me why all the photos I take end up blurry, I hid my hands in my lap. Because when I was twenty, I laughed into my pillow and I didn't know how to believe that this good thing is my life.

Because I stole peaches by the side of the road once just to prove to myself that I am still alive. Because I was so tired and I did not want to die but life seemed like such a tiresome thing. Because I know people who are phoenixes and I can't believe how easily they wipe off the ash on their wings. Because I love purple. Because I love the sea and because I love love. Because my heart thrashes in my chest and I have to laugh. Because some days tears just wouldn't come. Because I don't know where to put the guilt. Because I want to put joy everywhere. Because I am human. Because I want to leave this planet. Because my jokes are terrible but I am sure my poetry has made someone smile. Because I am still looking for permission. Because I have seen the constellations for the first time in my life three weeks ago and I didn't know what to feel. Because I failed failed failed. Because I fucking won. Because I, as Anka and Sinatra sang it, did it my way. Because I know honey and salt, too. Because I want to hold my best friend's hand and show her all the good in the world. Because I love all of my past lovers. Because I am afraid of being happy. Because I am afraid of being afraid. Because I want to do some good. Because some days I just want to pull all the shutters down. Because I know what kindness is and I haven't believed in humanity until I didn't have electricity and someone offered me a power bank. Because when I was five, I slammed into the corner of my house.

Because when I was seventeen, I loved every scar. Because there is poetry in humid summers and there is poetry in how you look when you are tired. Because I swear too much and smoke too much and I am still learning how to be happy. Because Hare Krishnas passed through my town once and I loved the music. Because I wanted to sing Ave Maria with a prayer community in the airport in Barcelona. Because I don't think I have ever been in love but I think I have always loved. Because I still have miles to go but I no longer sleep with a suitcase beside my bed. Because I let the world hold me for once and it did not let me fall. Because I have been cruel. Because I want to be kind. Because sun sets in the west but it would be such a trip if it set in the east, man. Because I believe in magic. Because truth is stranger than lies. Because I have kept strangers' secrets and enemies' secrets. Because I can't tell anyone so I tell everyone. Because the world can go on without me. But I don't want it to.

FLOWERS IN DESOLATE GROUND

Don't confuse kindness
for weakness.

Sometimes anger is kindness, too,
learning to let go and say: *No,*
I will love myself first.

The world doesn't want you angry,
it would be easier to just give and give carelessly
until there is nothing to come back home to,
and love is a roar and an echo
but you can't grow flowers in desolate ground.

So be kind and be patient but know that
you can love like spring and riot like summer
at the same time
and you can offer and want, at the same time.

When I beg you to be kind
(because the world is cruel enough as it is)
this is what I mean –

Love yourself first,
find your place under the sun and refuse to give it up,
fight fiercely and care even more so.

You are not simple,
you are a galaxy coming home to itself
and when they tell you that you can't love and be
furious –

bare your teeth

and open your heart.

THE HUNGER

I don't want to be an inspiration,
I want to be inspired.

I want to touch the night sky with my bare hands,
so what if it burns me?

I want the scorch mark reminders
of how I was brave,
of how I was more than these bones,
firmly rooted to the earth.

I want to know what Icarus thought
when he flew too close,

I want to know what hunger for the world
tastes like.

IF I HAVE TO FALL, I WILL SOAR FIRST

Girl, you are Icarus,
the wax is still dripping down your skin
and the sun breathes fire on your cheeks.

You are Icarus,
fearless and reckless and young and alive,
laughter like a roar,
mind like the ocean.

You are Icarus,
and they tell you that you will burn
because they don't know what to do with your shine.

But you are Icarus,
and so you tell them –
yes.

But first,
I will fly.

TO THE GIRL I NO LONGER HAVE TO BE BUT NOW WANT TO BE

This is your car crash symphony,

Do not ever apologize for the fury.

I have been starved under these stars,
could choke on this sugarcoat forgiveness
shit,
playing at pretty songs like I had forgotten,
waking up to discover that I had set the room on fire.

But I see you now, you with your
bloody hands and a songbird
for a heart. I see you.

I could never unsee you.

I used to apologize to our lovers,
and now I tell them it's useless,
you can't preach peace
to someone who is calling for war.

Fuck their pretty songs,
there is nothing to fix here.

And this fury?

This fury makes ancient things tremble.

The only thing I am sorry for is
that I ever said I was sorry,
thinking that this fight was never mine
because our song would sound like char
and taste like one too many bullets.
It would be
devastating. It would be
beautiful.

I mean, look at all this dried blood.
My head breaks open. I give birth
to war.

And it was the one thing that did me in, sent me
shouting through open windows, hurtling myself
at the world and demanding
that it take all of me.

This is pool mad black ink
storm hit
deliverance:

We will not be unmade.

YOU ARE YOUR OWN SAVIOR

I don't have a poem to write about a boy,
but I do have one about a girl.

I don't have a poem to write about how he touched
me and made me feel whole for a moment,
but I do have one about how I laughed in the face of
blood and broken teeth,
how I pronounced myself so whole that not even the
universe could
deny me.

I don't have a poem to write about how he kissed the
reckless scar on my knee,
but I have one about how I ran so fast my lungs nearly
burst
and how, when they found me on the pavement,
I was laughing through tears.

I don't have a poem to write about how the crown
shone upon his pretty head,
about how, when he kissed my thighs,
he swore he would give me an empire.

But I do have a poem to write about how I rose out of
ruins
and how Rome burned
beneath my feet.

YOU ARE ALL MY SISTERS

Here is to the burning girls:

Illuminating every night they set foot in,
smiles sharp and minds on fire, stubbornly surviving
with their tongues uncoiled as if to say –
Now that I've found my freedom,
you can never take it from me.

Here is to the girls who fight back:

Those who know the rule of being the smaller one
in a fight,
just hold on until your enemy gets tired and then
finish them off;
I love your blood-stained teeth, lionhearts
(conquerors have nothing on you.)

Here is to the soft girls:

The brave ones who never let calloused hands
turn their hearts bitter,
those who know better,
who know how to turn all this violence into love;
The truly fearless ones.

And here is to us, here is to the almighty girls:

Give us coal
and we will give you gold.

NO FEAR

Is this what life is like
when you can breathe
without fear?

Is this how people feel,
loving and laughing and
waking up in cotton?

See, I am a war child and
while I do love the blue sky,
mine has always been red.

I forgot that magic can come
as a cry of seagulls,
and not a shadow garden in blooming July,
I forgot that people are born differently,
love first,
scars later.

So this poem is the opposite of a battle cry,
this is the victory,
a revelation at 3am with
wounded feet -

I am sorry for making your sheets
smell like war,
but how else would you know
the price of
peace?

BONES

I don't have a romantic bone in my body?

No,
all the bones
in my body
are romantic.

I pry sorrow from my lips
and it spills like wine,
like a lover
that I cannot name.

I dig deep to uncover
hidden earth in my chest,
hoping that there is something in the light
that will let me hold it.

I drown in the empty pool and gurgle
saltwater,
and because no one ever told me about the soft kind,
I dream of revolutions with my hands in my hair.

I choke on myths and tales and look,
Persephone is just walking down a long road,
standing up where Icarus fell,
and none of us know how to be sorry for
the crushing depth.

No, I do not have a single romantic bone in my body -
I have *more*.

No one has ever taught me the art
of wishing things with
half a heart.

I either burn
or I decay.

DON'T LET THEM KILL THEIR HERO

They always kill their heroes,
Andromedas chained to rocks and Icari
falling to the bottom of the ocean.

There is no beast wilder than fear.

So if you must be a hero,
be unconquerable, be fearless,

Spread immortality across your skin like armor
(*Achilles had armor, too, and he died*,
yes but darling, Achilles wasn't you.)

Weave threads of life through your heart,
follow them when the world is raw red
(*Wasn't there a hero who followed a thread?*
Yes, but Theseus never knew the strength you carry
in your bones.)

So if you must be a hero
of people who will ruin you out of fear,
be a *goddess*.

And when they come with their nooses and their
torches,
laugh at them and say:
this hero will not be unmade.

NO SHAME

unlearn shame
like a false belief
that no longer serves you.

bloom wild and
bloom p u r e,

even if your knees are
            dirty.

SECOND SKIN

Here is what I know:

The world keeps telling me that I should
find a boy to love me and not ask why,
they don't tell him how to love me,
as if I could ever settle for scraps from
someone else's table.

I need to sit down and shut up,
cross my legs and smile real pretty,
they don't like it when I walk with my head held high
and
when I sit like all the world is my throne.

My words should be soft and my lips loving,
how dare I vow to take my revenge,
how dare I (*just a girl*) feel fury like second skin?

Be soft,
be small,
don't take up space.

You've got a sailor's mouth on you, he says.

Oh baby, but my tongue is poetry.

IF NOT A MONUMENT, THEN A POEM

I want to feel it,
I want to feel how my existence touched you.

I want statues for this feeling and
I want songs in place of mirror shards,

And I want the world to know that I was here,
that these are my fingerprints on every miracle,
my scorch marks on every disaster and still,
that it was my own heart that brought me back,
that it was my own hands that held me up.

I want the right words to show what it feels like to be
the underdog
and then win,
in spite of vicious voices,
and the one booming in my head –
telling me to stop.

I want the world to know that I have so many regrets
but never stopping when everyone wanted me to
is not one of them.

I want a continent for this desire,
for this pure want,
for the hunger burning like a forest fire,
for the courage I had when I squared my shoulders
and proclaimed – *I want.*

I want the world to paint my heartbeat across its walls
because I was here,
and I was small and I was insignificant and I dreamt
until I was more.

I want the universe to know exactly how bright I
shine
because I used to be a piece of rubble
and look at me now.

SIMFONIJA

I ima pjesama koje traže da se napiješ,
srce koje puca po šavovima,
i eto, to je ono što imam,
čak i kada nemam ništa.

Pričaj mi o tome kako smo lomili čaše
bježeći od samih sebe,
ali ritam nas je našao,
stranac s poznatim glasom.

Jer ovi prostori su prokleti i
jedino smo tugovali,
čuvali veselje u poderanim džepovima kaputa
za neke sretnije dane
koji još uvijek nisu došli.

Voljela bih da znam note
pa da napišem simfoniju,
kunem se da bi vam slomila srce
i vratila ga na mjesto do kraja stranice.

Nema golotinje do one kada govoriš svojim jezikom,
i pišeš svojim jezikom,
i živiš svojim jezikom,
pa u ogledalu ne vidiš odraz svojeg tijela -
nego svojeg naroda.

Provela sam život bježeći
i voljela bih da znam kako
ostati.

Voljela bih da nisam stranac
onima koje volim,
voljela bih da napišem tu jebenu simfoniju,
tu prokletinju od boli koja se prenosi s koljena na
koljeno,
tu svetinju od veselja koja se pronalazi samo kada
zaslužiš.

Pa da tom jednom simfonijom otkrijem baš sve,
i ožiljke i pobjede,
pa da zaprepastim svijet da padne u čudo,
da *postane* čudo.

Da barem jednom na kraju strane ne otkrijem mrak,
da barem jednom od tuge naučim
kako iz ničega
stvoriti
svjetlo.

SYMPHONY
Translated to English

And there are songs that call for you to get drunk,
heart bursting at the seams,
and that is what I have,
even when I have nothing.

Tell me about how we smashed glasses
running away from ourselves,
but the rhythm found us,
a stranger with a familiar voice.

Because these parts are cursed and
the only thing we ever did was grieve,
keeping our joy in ripped coat pockets
for some better days
that still haven't come.

I wish I knew notes
so I can write a symphony,
I swear it would break your heart
and put it back by the end of the page.

There is no bareness more revealing than when you
speak in your language,
and write in your language,
and live in your language,
so in the mirror you do not see the reflection of your
body -

but of your people.

I have spent my whole life running
and I wish I knew how to
stay.

I wish I wasn't a stranger
to the ones I love,
I wish I could write that fucking symphony,
that fucking pain handed down from generation
to generation,
that relic of joy that you find
only when you
deserve it.

And with that one symphony - uncover absolutely
everything,
the scars and the victories,
and leave the world wondering,
turn it
into a wonder.

And at least once,
I wish that, at the end of the page,
instead of discovering darkness,
I learn from sorrow
how to create light
out of nothing
at all.

PRETTY

I don't care about pretty.

Show me what you look like at 3am
in an Autobahn gas station parking lot,
fluorescents spilling over you.

They have the uncanny ability to pool
in your collarbone when your legs are the only things
touching the ground.

They call this a modern migration,
how we dream of flying but forget to take maps
and fall anyway.

Show me what you look like with wind-whipped
cheeks, deep red creases,
zebra-striped socks
(the only clean thing on you right now.)

I think that is when I fell in love,
when you looked at me over a three euro hamburger
and said:
Fuck, but I love feeling like shit with you.

Show me what you look like in the early morning.

Been chasing these dreams for a long time,
you've got it all figured out as you fasten your tie.
You kiss me in the doorway and our love still tastes

like June evenings with my feet in your lap,
a road to nowhere.

Show me what you look like when you are
a little tired, when the world has been unkind to you.

I don't care about the ugly,
I don't care about your dark parts.
If I could, I would beg just one answer off this endless
sky –
I'd beg it to tell me that we are more
than just sum of the thorns
we got cut on.

I don't care about pretty.

Pretty is not where the real beauty happens.
It happens when you smile, your feet
on my dashboard and bruised knees.
It happens when the angles of my face are too sharp
and you love me anyway.
It happens when we are tired and wrecked and
this isn't life,
this is a third category tornado -
the ground doesn't know how to stop trembling.

Maybe one too many bad days get you here,
to seeing beauty in the wretched.
Maybe that's what happens when we are constantly
on the verge of something
and always falling short.
I wish we didn't know tragedy so intimately.

I wish we had known kindness
before cruelty.

So I don't care about pretty.

Show me all your mismatched parts.

Let me turn you into art anyway.

ANTISEPTIC

You smell like antiseptic cream when I see you
and it leaves stains on my skin.

Some nights I think that I could combust into
neon green and pink, something that hurts to look at
and I think - good.
Good, beauty is overrated.
I want to be so ugly that it makes you want to
know me. I want to bare my scars and tell you to write
a story for every single one.
We are band-aid people, using colorful ones
to make ourselves feel less sad.

But we never do. You felt like a sojourn and tasted like
swallowing gravel. I still remember
how my cheek on the pavement felt.

My best memories always come with pain and it is not
because I think that I deserve to suffer (which I do)
but because I know happy endings are not happy at
all.

We crave them anyway. Did I say that you smell like
antiseptic already? I forget sometimes. I have always
hated green hospital walls so put me in your car
but don't take me to the emergency room.
I would do the same for you.
Don't call it love if it's just patching the lonely.

It is incredible what tales humans will spin out of
the basic desire to survive. We sit with our thighs
pressed together and I say: I am not good at this.
Can't you taste the mourning when you kiss me?

All I taste is sunlight. Even if it feels like red hot rage
most days. It is sunlight to me.
When you have spent enough time in the shadows,
light hurts your eyes.

We are still trying. I can see it in how you smile with
your sunglasses on, white teeth but it never reaches
your eyes. There is a cage inside your chest and you
pound at it. When you look in the mirror,
you do not recognize yourself.

They call it healing. We do not call it at all.

It takes time to come home. It takes more to believe
that you even deserve to.

VICTORY

Girl, for every time they told you no -
roar - YES.

For every time you opened your mouth to speak and
they talked over you,
for every time they pushed you into a corner
expecting you to give up,

For every time your laugh was too loud and your jokes
too crude and "you should be a lady" -

tell them to fuck off.

Slam your fist against the table and be the queen
I know you to be,
refuse to stand in the corner because, if anything,
you were born for the light.

Laugh like it's the last thing you'll do,
curse like a sailor until you can get the ropes to leave
marks of survival on your skin.

And when they smile
when they tell you that
the world is going to shut you up eventually,
tell them -

It tried
and I left its teeth bloody.

BARE

i am bare skin and sea salt
with my feet in the atlantic
ocean;
when i close my eyes,
i dream of shipwrecks.

watch me grow and watch me
bloom -
these bones are a house
burned down,
this heart is all freedom.

one day i am going to touch the sky
and rip it in two;
i am a broken promise and i am
innocence
found in the dirt.

these ribs are what you bruised your
knuckles on,
these lips are just leaking poetry.

and i've been loving until i started
burning
and now i am writing eulogies
out of
apologies.

constellations will scream my name.

JUNE 11

June was kind to me.

I choked on the freedom caught in my throat
and for the first time,
I felt flowers bloom
in the empty spaces
between my ribs.

Everything was soft and all that which had hurt me
brought me back to life
in the end.

I was tired of my heavy heart and my heavy heart
was tired of me.

Every ugly thing turned beautiful in the end.

And this was not happiness, this was
peace
as I tripped over words, tripped over my own hands.
The apples lay rotten in my palms and I stood,
having had it with a lifetime full of violence,
dirty songs and
my fingers,
dirtier still.

I held my heart as a ripe fruit and saw it
for what it was –
I called the bruises bruises,
I called the fury fury,

And I was not ashamed,
I was saved.

The sea turned into a mirror
and I liked what I saw.

LIVES

Lives stick to me like the cherry lip gloss I find in my
grandmother's attic, right by the christening dress,
by the first braid I had cut off like shedding my skin.

I was so many things in so little time.

I was fury,
sweltering hot blistering rage summer kind of feral,
sweat pooling in your collarbone and skin sticky with
want. There was no ink-stained grace in how I forged
my own gold out of blood.
No one wanted to keep kissing the girl who only
spoke of death, anyway.

(They pull you in and ruin you with their crazy, they
do.)

I was the green line dripping down your family tree.
It's all in the genes, your mother's eyes, your father's
nose, how you put your fingers to the piano and Earth
shifts beneath my feet.
But pain, too, huh, did you notice that?

When you burn someone's house down you aren't just
destroying the walls.
You are destroying a history, too.
So put down the matches. Walk away.
This is not yours to ruin.

I was crazy, dirty, absofuckinglutely insane love. The
kind you only get when you've got a desperate soul
and don't know what to do with it anymore.
You've got to pour your heart into *something*, right?
But no one told you when to stop pouring.
When you bleed out, they step over your body
on the sidewalk.
Wildflowers will grow from your bones.

I was ephemeral, a fleeting moment in time,
now you see it now you don't, blink and you'll miss it.
Keep good eyes on the road and don't look back, find
me when you hear the music that wasn't supposed to
be there. *More* feels like champagne bubbles in your
chest.
Your heart is a riot and you've got grease-stained
fingertips but your hands always looked good to me.

I was a peach orchard once, I'm sure. I made
something grow, light attracts light and man, oh man,
did the moths love me.

I was the summer you stole your first kiss, I was
a swelling symphony. I made something look beautiful
and my trees trapped sunlight.

I was a peach orchard once, I'm sure.
You don't forget that kind of joy.

It always makes the shadows a little less terrifying.

SWEET

As with everything,
you need to unlearn what you have been told,
what they preached to you with conviction that
seemed honest enough to move mountains.

We are all roundabouts and we do learn,
we do make a home out of these bones,
but we always come back to ourselves in the end.

At the end of your life, you are memories
so my grandmother pours an extra sugar
into my coffee,
smiles because I can't lie to *her*, sees behind
the façade of jokingly saying that
I take my coffee sweet
because my life is bitter enough.

Her eyes are all mischief, the girl who dove into
the Danube from the tallest branch, still has scars
to prove it
(and maybe I am trying to learn from her).

I laugh, I say, "That's too sweet, grandma."

The girl returns,
smiles as she cuts through the lies.

"Nothing is too sweet for you."

(*You deserve sweeter.*)

PEBBLES AND WISHBONES

You are not a fairytale,
you didn't fall out of a storybook and
started walking.

Of course you are not pretty to wish on,
there is no ink-stained grace to be found in the way
you crawled out of the raw, the black and blue, the
bruised,
the holy
history
and fell on the sidewalk.

No,
you are not a fairytale.

You are *a myth*.

Behold, how we defied gods and they left our hearts
swollen,
how we loved with a passion that left our mouth full
of sand and glass,
how we never knew that we couldn't be stars
so we swallowed them whole.

You are a testament to ruins and palaces turned into
rubble,
flowers growing out of concrete,
the thick air and marble statues and quiet inside,
quiet inside,
you've seen it all and you can't unsee it now.

Fairytales are for children,
a long road and a crossroad choice between the good
and the good,
wishbones and fairy dust woven into your hair;

Myths are every pebble buried under your skin
walking the road barefoot,
a crossroad choice between the bad and the worse,
battle cries and knowing that you are something more
but never getting the chance to understand what.

You are a myth and so you must take back what they
tore out of you,
take it all, take the good and the obscure and the ugly
and forge your own gold out of it;

Take it back with trembling hands and a heavy heart
but for the love of God,
take it back.

Cut your story into marble, every line and every
breath.
Take it back and write it into the stars.

Write:
how I danced,
how I fought,
how I devoured,

how I survived.

ABOUT THE AUTHOR

Lana Rafaela Cindric was born on April 23rd, 1996 in Zagreb, Croatia. Her birthday is on the World Book Day, which she reminds herself of when she feels insecure about her writing.

Unfortunately, she still hasn't achieved her life goal of running into a waddle of penguins screaming at the top of her lungs but she is very optimistic about it.